A Pictorial History of RODE

The Somerset Village where Mr. Whicher had his suspicions

by

Peter Harris

British Library Cataloguing-in-Publication-Data: a catalogue record of this book is held by the British Library.

First Printing 2011

ISBN No. 978-0-9564073-7-5

Published in Great Britain by:

THE HEART OF RODE COMMITTEE
Reg. charity no. 1128078

c/o Camden MSS
Barrow Farm, Rode, Frome, Somerset. BA11 6PS

Layout and design by Camden Studios.

Printed by Salisbury Printing Co. Ltd.

NOTE: the colour used on the cover is Royal Blue. King George III challenged clothmakers nationwide to produce a material suitable for royal use. The clothiers of Scutt's Bridge Mill in Rode created a cloth of this rich blue colour and it was selected for a robe for Queen Charlotte, the long-suffering wife of George III. The colour became known as 'Royal Blue' and King William IV issued a certificate authorizing its sale by that name.

Contents

Preface 4

Introduction 5

Map 7

St. Lawrence 8
The Bell Inn 10
Clay Lane House 11
Rode Filling Station & Café 12
The Sportsman & Bradford Road 13
Christchurch 14
Rode Hill 16
Langham Place 17
Rode Hill House 18
Mogg Hill 19
Rode Bridge 20
Rode Manor 22
Rode Tropical Bird Gardens 24
The Miller's House & River Baptisms 25
Barrow Farm 26
Lower Street 28
Townsend Street 30
Townsend 32
Rockabella House 33
Scutt's Bridge & Mill 34
The Corner House 36
The Cross Keys Inn & Fussell's Brewery 37
The Reading Rooms 38
George W. Stokes' Store 40
High Street & The Pound 42
The Green & Marsh Road 44
The War Memorial 46

Appendices

1. Rode Time Line 48
2. Whitaker & Noad Family Lines 50
3. Batten & Pooll Family Lines 51
4. Bibliography 52

Preface

Like many people today my work, as a naval constructor with the Ministry of Defence, often required me to move my home, and I came to Rode expecting to be here for only three or four years. As it happened I have been able to stay in the village for what is now half my life. So, although some may still class me as a blow-in, I now feel this is where I belong.

My interest in village history was sparked by our late chairman of the parish council, Paul Stacey, who would tell intriguing tales of previous inhabitants as he led groups on history walks around the village. Membership of the parish council and other village organisations broadened my knowledge of historic village documents and events. I became involved in history related activities, e.g. 'beating the bounds', digitising the graveyard records and looking after the Queen Victoria Jubilee Clock.

The latter led me to write a history of the Clock, as part of the agreement with the Heritage Lottery Fund for a grant towards its refurbishment. The word then seemed to spread that I was interested in village history and I have since been given or allowed to copy a wide variety of old documents and pictures. I have always been keen that this information should be accessible to all those interested, so when asked if I would prepare this pictorial history I was delighted to give it a try.

I thank all those who have assisted me in the preparation of this booklet and in particular those who have so generously provided me with the results of their research; Dawna Pine, Harry Hopkins, Brian Foyston and Sidney Fussell. I also thank Adam Harris for his encouragement and assistance with its publication.

Peter Harris
September 2011

Introduction

The book is a collection of pictures depicting Rode in the past. They are arranged to provide a pleasant walk round this attractive village, thus enabling the reader to see and understand some of the changes that have taken place in the last 150 years. The following brief history of the village, together with the supporting time line (appendix 1), provide an overall background, which the reader may find helpful in understanding the context of each picture.

A Brief History

The roots of Rode stretch back to before the Norman invasion. A settlement developed here possibly because it was a convenient crossing point of the river Frome and even in those early times the community was harnessing the power of the river. The Domesday Book records three manors in Rode and several mills, the latter being of greater value than the three at Frome. There are today several distinct areas of settlement in Rode, and this may be a reflection of the complex historic manorial arrangements. Close to the old church of St Lawrence are also the earthworks of buildings said to have been abandoned as a result of fire or plague.

In the 13th century one of the manors was in the hands of the St. Maur family and the name still survives at Seymour's Court south of St. Lawrence church. At that time Rode was of sufficient importance in the area for the King to grant Laurence de St. Maur permission to hold a weekly market in Rode on Thursdays and a fair on St. Margaret's Day (20 July). Other names in the village remind one of the medieval manorial and agricultural systems of those times; Green Park (Cottages and Lane), the Lord of the Manor's private hunting ground; Southfield (House), one of the customary 3 arable fields; and Rode Common, where villagers grazed their animals.

From the 16th to 19th centuries the West Country woollen cloth trade had a major impact on the village. The corn mills were initially extended to include fulling stocks, then as new technology developed, they were enlarged, or new ones built, to accommodate spinning, weaving and dyeing machinery. In some cases they ended up as large 4-storey steam-powered factories with many employees. Most of these buildings have now disappeared, but some of the houses built by the prosperous owners of these mills do remain. The estates of the leading families can be traced down through the generations using the simplified family line trees at appendices 2 & 3.

It was towards the end of this period that Samuel Kent, a factory inspector, came to live at Rode Hill House, with his family. The murder of his young son, in 1860, and the confession of his daughter, Constance, made Rode the talk of the nation and the controversy and public interest in the crime continues to this day. At the same time Henry Fussell, a hard working village baker and grocer, had just taken on a new venture, with the purchase of the Cross Keys Inn. He and his descendants were to develop this modest establishment into a brewing and farming business, which became the major employer and land owner in the village through much of the 20th C. Now, with the business closed and most of the buildings replaced by houses, Rode has become much quieter and, perhaps because of this, a much sought after village in which to live.

Village Names and Boundaries

During the 18th and 19th centuries the spelling of the village name was "Road". This gave rise to much confusion and misdirection of mail and other deliveries intended for the village so, in 1919, the village held a meeting and decided to revert to the pre 1700 spelling "Rode". The latter spelling has been adopted throughout this book, irrespective of the date of events described.

Also at that time, the county boundary passed through the middle of the village. Most of Rode was in Somerset, but the area between Lower St., High St. and Rode Hill was in the parish of North Bradley in Wiltshire (see map on page 7), and hence under the jurisdiction of that county's constabulary. The boundary was moved north and Rode and Rode Hill united within Somerset in 1937.

Map of the Walk

THE WALK round the village starts at St. Lawrence Church on the Frome to Trowbridge road. There is a small amount of parking at the church. It may also be possible to leave your car in the car-park of the Bell Inn near the church, but check with the landlord first.

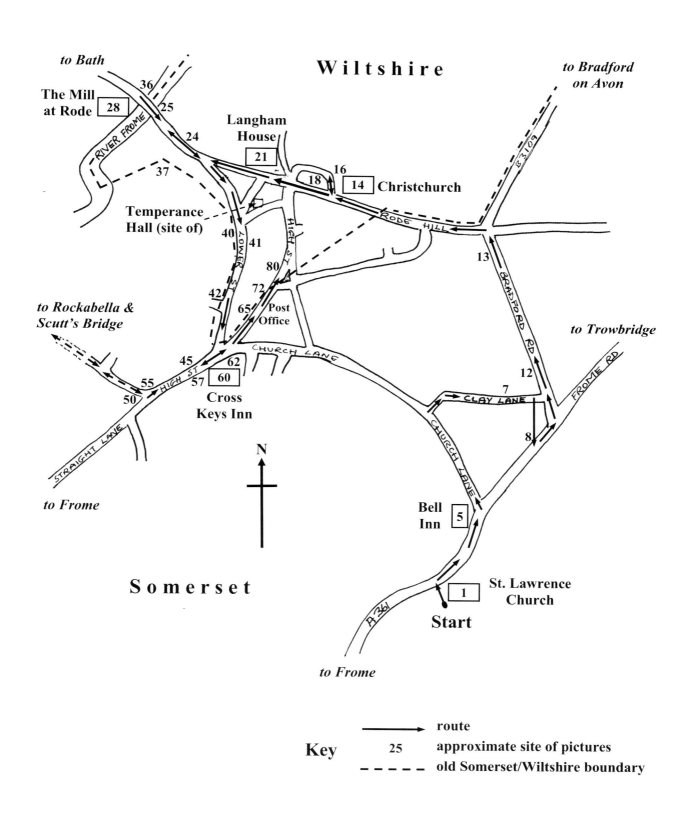

1. St. Lawrence
c1870

Mention was made in the Domesday Survey of a priest named Rumbal serving Frome and Rode but the first priest recorded at St. Lawrence was John de Thorenden in 1226. The present church of St. Lawrence is thought to date from the 15th C. but the signs of a smaller building were found during a major renovation in 1873.

The absence of the central heating chimney to the right of the tower indicates that the photograph above was taken before the renovation. In the field in front of the church are the remains of an earlier settlement.

There are some fine chest tombs in the churchyard and the interior of the church is well worth seeing but you will need to get a key from the churchwardens.

The addition of the vestry (below, left front corner) was a major part of the 1873 renovations.

2. St. Lawrence
c1900
by Wilkinson

Road Church.

*3. Clypping
the Church
c1850 by
W. W. Wheatley*

The origins of the clypping ceremony are thought to be pre-Christian, with the purpose of creating a protective ring to keep out evil and drive the devil away. The painting was presented to Rev. Crofton, rector of Rode-cum-Woolverton from 1888 to 1894, by one of his parishioners. His son, Major Geoffrey Crofton gave the painting to the churchwardens in 1952, in memory of his father, and it now hangs in St. Lawrence.

The fine lych gate (shown below) was also built during the 1873 renovations. Unfortunately it was demolished by a car in 1966.

*4. St. Lawrence
c1918
by Wilkinson*

Road Church. — From the battlements of the Tower of this Church Charles II surveyed the country round after his defeat at the Battle of Worcester. Hence the place is called "The King's Chair".

FROM St. Lawrence turn right along the Frome Road towards Trowbridge.

5. The Bell Inn c1900

You come to the Bell Inn at the junction of Church Lane and the Frome Road. The building is listed as early 19th C. and was recorded in the 1839 Tithe Apportionment as the Bell Inn, owned by James Budd and occupied by John Dervell.

Across Church Lane from The Bell is Westlands (15 Frome Road), built in the 1860s by well known Rode builder, Edward Silcocks (Silcox). The adjoining cottages were built almost one hundred years earlier as indicated by a stone plaque on 17 Frome Road, inscribed "CWR 1777".

A comparison of these views shows little changed over the years except the addition of the bus shelter and the telephone posts.

6. The Bell Inn c1955 by Fitzwilliam

FROM here, follow Church Lane and turn right into Clay Lane.

*7. Clay Lane House
c1910*

Along the lane on the left is Clay Lane House (2 Clay Lane).

The 1792 map of the enclosure of Rode Common shows a house on this site, which was owned by Jonathan Noad, the prosperous Rode wool merchant and mill owner.

By 1839, the property had passed to his daughter-in-law, Emily Noad and then in 1856 to her son Arthur Mayne Noad.

The house was probably renovated by Edward Silcocks c1860 as it has his characteristic stone brackets to the gutters, ears on the stone window surrounds and stonework over the door.

By 1881, Benjamin Hancock, dairyman, was living there. At some time during his residency, he scratched his name in one of the downstairs windows of the house and it is still there.

Prior to 1919, the property was owned by Charles

Humphrey Carden Noad who inherited A. M. Noad's estate including the disused brickyard on Rode Common. He sold the property in 1919 to Percy John Fussell and by 1957 it belonged to his widow, Ida Fussell. The house still retains many old features, including the flagstone floor in the dining room, beams and stone mullioned windows.

*CONTINUE almost to the end of Clay Lane and turn right along the footpath into Church Fields.
At the end of the path follow the road to its junction with the Trowbridge Road.*

8. Aerial view of Rode Filling Station and Café c1970

In the 1970s and 80s this was the site of Rode Filling Station and Cafe. Later the cafe was replaced by Rode Garden Machinery Centre.

RODE CAFE

(Situated on the A 361)
5 miles between Frome & Trowbridge.
Tel. Beckington 454

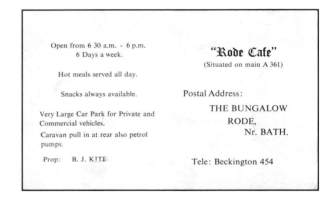

Open from 6 30 a.m. - 6 p.m.
6 Days a week.

Hot meals served all day.

Snacks always available.

Very Large Car Park for Private and
Commercial vehicles.

Caravan pull in at rear also petrol
pumps.

Prop: B. J. KITE

"Rode Cafe"

(Situated on main A 361)

Postal Address:

THE BUNGALOW
RODE,
Nr. BATH.

Tele: Beckington 454

9. Postcard of the Cafe c1970

10. Filling Station c1980

11. Garden Machinery Centre c1980

TURN LEFT along the Trowbridge Road to its junction with the Bradford Road. Turn left again up the Bradford Road to The Sportsman/Clay Lane.

Behind the new houses of The Sportsman there is a converted barn (the building at bottom centre of this view). Since 1964 it has been Fussell's 'Sportsman' steakhouse, a Thai restaurant, and now is residential property. Clayfields (22 Bradford Road), adjoining the barn, was owned by Thomas Stevens in 1792 and by 1839 William Perks was owner and occupier. At the rear of Clayfields, there is a projecting semi-circular stair, much like the one at Vaggs Hill House near Tellisford. Clay pipes are thought to have been

12. Aerial view of Houses at Bradford Road/Clay Lane 1964

made on the property at one time, as many have been found in the garden behind the house. These old houses have large front gardens because when Rode Common was enclosed in 1792, the road was built well away from them. The strip of land between was allotted to the lord of the manor, Edward Andrews, and only later became part of the properties.

CONTINUE up the Bradford Road.

No. 6 (The Old Rectory) was built in the early 19th C and in 1874, when it was put up for sale, it was known as Rode Hill Villa. In 1920 it was purchased by the governors of Queen Anne's Bounty as a residence for the curate.

Nos. 2 and 4 Hillcrest Villas were built by Edward Silcocks for the Wilden sisters. They wanted them to look like one large house. For many years they were known as Moncrieff and McIver Villas.

13. Rode Rectory and Hill Crest Villas c1925 by Wilkinson

CONTINUE on up to the crossroads and turn left along Rode Hill. Pass the junction of Marsh Road,
continue down Rode Hill and cross the road where the footpath ends.

14. Christchurch
c1930
by Dafnis

On the right are Daubeney House and Christchurch House.

Rode Hill and the area between High Street and Lower Street were part of the parish of North Bradley in Wiltshire, as indicated by a parish boundary stone in the refuge on Rode Bridge.

Archdeacon Daubeney, vicar of North Bradley, was so concerned that some of his Rode Hill parishioners were attending St. Lawrence rather than walk 4 miles to their church in North Bradley, that he built Christ Church in 1824.

The unification of Rode and Rode Hill parishes, the decline in church attendances, the need for very expensive repairs and the proximity of St. Lawrence, led to the closure of Christ Church in 1995 and its conversion to a private residence.

From here, there was a splendid view across the Fairfield to the centre of Rode until the houses were built in the 1980s.

15. Rode from
Rode Hill
c1930
by Dafnis

TURN RIGHT just past Christchurch House in to Langham Place and proceed to the first house on the right.

16. Rode Hill School c1950

Rode Hill also had its own school, next to Christchurch in Langham Place. It was built by subscription in 1834 and could hold more than 75 children. Initially it was managed by the church and later became a "National school" run by the Government. It closed in 1922 when the population in Rode Hill had dropped to 177 and the remaining children were transferred to the Rode Wesleyan school.

For several decades the building was used by various organisations, including the Women's Institute before being demolished c1950. The lower part of the front of the school still remains, as the garden wall of The Stables (no. 19), Langham Place.

17. Rode Hill School c1925 by Wilkinson

RETRACE your steps to Rode Hill and continue down the hill.

18. Rode Hill Terrace 2011

The stone-fronted terrace on the right was built by Percy Fussell in 1938 for his brewery employees. Some of the stone came from the ruins of Rockabella House. Compare the arched window in the centre house with picture no. 51.

The detached brick houses, nos. 13 & 21 at each end of the terrace, were built at the same time for the brewery managers.

The brewery business increased rapidly in the early 1930s and Percy Fussell realised that more housing was needed in Rode to accommodate his expanding workforce. Additional housing was not really viable without a piped water supply, but having taken over chairmanship of the parish council from George W. Stokes, he was well placed to petition the District Council for a mains supply to be brought to the village.

CONTINUE down Rode Hill to Langham Place.

19. Rode Hill/ High Street Junction c1950

Now look across the junction with the High Street towards the Memorial Hall and compare it with the scene above. The first efforts to provide the Hall were taken by the Rode branch of the British Legion during WW2. Capt. W. S. Batten Pooll offered the land in 1946 at a peppercorn rent, but there was little money available and it was not until 1955 that the Hall was eventually provided by the National Council for Social Service at a rent of £13 per annum.

20. Langham Place c1918 by Wilkinson

Langham is thought to have been one of three manors in Rode. The cottage, left of centre above, was the home of May Woolley. Her father had been caretaker of the Reading Rooms soon after they were built in 1887 and she had been born in the small cottage between the Reading Rooms and the Cross Keys Inn.

21. Rode Hill House c1918 by Wilkinson

*22. Constance Kent
c1862*

Just below Langham Place is Langham (once Rode Hill) House. It was built c1795 for Thomas Whitaker Ledyard probably by T. Baldwin. He was the grandson of Thomas Whitaker the successful dyer and clothier of Rode Bridge.

In 1854 Samuel Kent, a factory inspector, and his family rented Rode Hill House. Six years later his infant son, (Francis) Saville, was cruelly murdered. The shocking crime gripped the attention of the nation and various theories were advanced as to who was responsible. Saville's step-sister, Constance, eventually admitted to the crime but her guilt or innocence is still hotly debated to this day. (Books relating to the crime can be found in the bibliography at appendix 4)

CONTINUE down Rode Hill to the lower gates of Langham House.

23. Rode Hill House c1900 by Wilkinson

In 1861, after the Kents had left the village, Rode Hill House was sold to Mr. Alfred Haynes, a woolstapler of Frome. He changed its name to Langham House and after two years also offered it for sale. The publicity for the auction described the property as: "A mansion house called Langham House together with coach-house, stable, garden, greenhouse, cottage, orchard, plantation, pleasure grounds and above 7 acres of superior pasture land."

CROSS the road with care just below the white railings, at the junction with Lower Street. Then look back across the road.

This part of Rode Hill is called Mogg Hill. The houses across the road have developed over many years from a group of eight or more weavers' cottages. They were owned by Edward West, a tailor, in 1805 and by his son in 1841.

24. Mogg Hill c1900 by Wilkinson

CONTINUE down the hill to Rode Bridge.

25. The Miller's House c1900

The Miller's House was built soon after Henry Whitaker established a dye house and cloth workshop here c1700. The business was very successful and continued through several generations. There were extensive mills and workshops behind the house and in the field opposite - all gone now. The elegant coach house and stable block were added later.

In 1768 Thomas Whitaker, who by then was running the dyeing business at Rode Bridge, agreed a 10 year bond to keep the bridge in good repair. Some time later plans were drawn up to widen the bridge, but were never carried out.

26. Rode Bridge c1900

CROSS the bridge, but don't miss the county and parish boundary stones in the central refuge.

27. Rode Bridge
Mill c1880
by P. Coard

There has probably been a mill on this site since before Domesday. 16th C. documents record tucking and gryst mills at this end of the bridge leased to the Pyarde family by the owners Richard Bamfield followed by Sir Walter Hungerford. The current building was added c1800, but the attached house shown in the above picture is probably older. In 1808 it was described as a woollen factory with adjoining fulling and gryst mill. With the decline of the woollen trade in the 19th C. the premises reverted to a corn mill until its closure at the end of the century.

28. Rode Bridge Mill in use as a corn mill c1900

NOW from the Mill, take a moment to look across at the park land between the roads
to Woolverton and Tellisford.

Manor House, Road.

29. Rode Manor c1900 by Wilkinson (now demolished)

30. Rode Manor Gardens c1900 by Wilkinson

These fields, which are private property, were once part of Northfield, one of three large open communal fields of medieval Rode.

In 1737 Mr Andrews, a Bristol merchant, acquired the manor of Rode and built a large house at the top of the hill, which he called Northfield House.

By the early 1800s, the house and land had been bought by brothers Henry Batten and Thomas Pooll.

Their great-nephew, Robert Pooll Langford inherited it in 1861 as a minor, on condition he adopted his benefactor's name. He greatly enlarged the house, to what is shown above, and renamed it Rode Manor.

The Batten Poolls were keen gardeners and developed beautiful gardens, water features and wooded areas around the house.

31. Rode Manor and Gardens c1935

32. Rode Manor and Gardens c1935

33. Rode Manor Demolition c1955

Robert Pooll Henry Batten Pooll died in 1930 and his son Captain Walter Batten Pooll inherited the property. After his death in 1955, the contents of the house were sold off, fittings were stripped out and it was demolished.

Donald and Betty Risdon bought the grounds in 1961 to develop into a tropical bird garden. The Garden opened in 1962 and became a great attraction as the varieties of birds and other entertainments increased from year to year. When Donald Risdon died a new owner could not be found and Bird Gardens closed in 2000. The site has since been developed into a small group of private houses.

A few of the Manor House buildings still remain. The building seen above, at the centre behind the demolished buildings, was used for the Bird Gardens (see below) and it is now incorporated into one of the residential properties.

34. Tropical Bird Gardens c1965

TURN AROUND and look across the river.

35. Rode Bridge
c1890

These views give glimpses of the extensive dye houses and workshops that once existed behind the Miller's House and in front of it on the other side of the road.

In the picture below William Wheatley captured the moment his wife, Emma, was baptised in 1843. Baptisms in the river continued until 1901.

36. The Baptising 1843 by W. W. Wheatley

RETRACE your steps over the bridge and up Mogg Hill.

37. Barrow House
c1880
by P. Coard

On the right in the field below is Barrow Farm. The present house was built in 1997 on the site of a much older one, which fell into disrepair c1890. Parts of the old structure have been retained including a window on the north wall.

The brook by the side of the house (now diverted) marked the boundary between Somerset and Wiltshire.

The footpath from Mogg Hill to Townsend used to run from the gate, straight across the front of the house and over the field to Rockabella Hill. This too was diverted when the new house was built and pond made.

38. The ruins of Barrow Farm in 1986

CONTINUE up Mogg Hill and turn right into Lower Street.

39. The Batch
c1900
by Wilkinson

On the left, in the angle between Halfpenny Lane and Farthing Row, are the remains of the Temperance Hall, where the inquest into Saville Kent's murder was held. This area of Lower Street was once called the Batch and Batch Cottage, no. 24, may have been the Beehive, a village alehouse.

In the 1860s, no. 25 was a bakery and grocers shop owned by James Morgan, the parish constable who, with police constable Urch, was summoned to search for the missing Saville Kent. James Morgan's granddaughter married William Towsey, who ran the shop in the early 1900s. It is said that he had been a sailor (and had sailed round Cape Horn), a farmer and a builder before becoming a shopkeeper.

40. Mr. Towsey's
Shop
c1905

CONTINUE along Lower Street.

The window of this shop at no. 18, Bellsburn, can still be seen standing out from the front of the building, although the door and porch have been replaced by an oval window. In 1843, the property was occupied by Henry Osborne and it consisted of a house, bakehouse, outbuildings, yard and garden.

In the 18th C. Lower Street was called Frog Street, no doubt because of the open stream that ran along the west side of the road. The stream comes from Moberley Pond beyond St. Lawrence, through the village to the river Frome at Barrow Farm. It has been covered in for many years and runs in a culvert under the pavement, gardens and houses.

In the past there have been some serious floods in the village, but a flood prevention scheme was undertaken as part of the development of the Old Brewery.

CONTINUE along Lower Street to its junction with High Street and turn right.

43. Townsend
Street
c1900

In the 19th C., this part of the High Street used to be called Townsend Street . On the left is Southfield House, which was extensively developed from three cottages in 1806 by Jonathan Noad. He gave the house to his eldest son Thomas Whitaker Noad. It later passed to Arthur Mayne Noad, a retired naval officer, a church warden and much respected village benefactor.

Part of the Rode, Rode Hill and Woolverton joint celebrations for the coronation of King George V was a parade of residents, led by the organising committee and accompanied by the brass band, from Townsend to Christchurch for a service of thanksgiving. Afternoon sports and other entertainments were held at Langham Fields, followed by dancing until dusk.

44. Coronation
Parade
1911

CONTINUE along High Street.

*45. The George
Inn
c1920*

On the right is 15 High Street, formerly an inn called The George. The building is 17th and late 18th C. and it was owned by Jonathan Noad when he made his will in 1809. The Inn remained in the Noad family until it was sold in 1877. Throughout that time it was occupied and run by William Smith and family.

CONTINUE along High Street.

*46. Townsend
c1910*

On the left, 6 and 8 High Street, together with The Old Ebenezer behind them, are thought to have once been part of a Benedictine priory. The ceiling beams of no. 8 have two carved wooden bosses in the form of a Tudor rose and the head of the devil. Further along on the left, is Rode School. The school was built by the Methodists and opened in 1860. By 1880 there were 136 children on the register, the highest number to date.

47. Townsend c1900

Opposite the school, there was a row of five 17th C. cottages. Only two remain, the others having been demolished in the late 1950s to make space for the extension of no. 5.

48. Townsend c1930

CONTINUE along High Street to its junction with the Mead.

49. Mayfield House
c1955
by Fitzwilliam

Beyond the school is Mayfield House. It is thought to date from the late 18th C. but nothing is known of who built it or its early history. Mrs Ann Bailey lived there in 1856 and she was left a life interest in it by her brother Henry Batten Pooll when he died in 1861. The adjoining factory is thought to be early 19th C. In 1839 it was reported as having a 16 hp steam engine and employing 50 people.

Opposite is Merfield Lodge, on the original entrance drive to Merfield House. The latter, situated in a clump of beech trees to the South, was built c1808 by Jonathan Noad, the successful woollen merchant.

50. Townsend
from the gates of
Merfield Lodge
c1910

IF you wish to extend your walk across the fields to the sites of Rockabella House and Scutt's Bridge Mill turn right, past the gates of Merfield Lodge, towards The Mead and then proceed straight ahead down the steep path called Rockabella Lane. For those wishing to keep to the paved way turn to page 35

51. Rockabella House c1930

In the small wood at the bottom of the hill are a few low stone walls and heaps of rubble, all that remains of Rockabella House and its adjoining mill. Thomas Noad lived and worked here before his death in 1760. He left his estate and cloth-making business to his adopted son, Jonathan Noad, who continued to live here with his wife, Sally, until he built and moved in to Merfield House.

52. Merfield House 2010

CONTINUE through the kissing gate on the left and follow the path beside the bed of the mill stream to Scutt's Bridge.

53. Scutt's Bridge

Scutt's Bridge is an old pack horse bridge, carrying the medieval track between Woolverton and Rode across the river Frome. The bridge would have been the main access for wool coming from the Mendips in the west to Rode on the east of the river.

200 metres upstream is a weir and to the left the mill stream, once spanned by Scutt's Bridge Mill. It was thought to be the last water-powered woollen mill in the area when it closed in 1904. Over the years the building became a picturesque ruin before it was demolished in 1974.

54. Scutt's Bridge Mill from the Northwest c1900 — note the pig

NOW retrace your steps to the High Street.

*55. Townsend
looking North
c1900
by Wilkinson*

On the left of the above picture is the walnut tree under which Wesley is said to have preached in 1746. The tree fell down in 1922 but a piece was saved and used as a plaque (now in the Methodist School) commemorating Wesley's visit. The picture also shows the school bell-tower and spire, which was removed c1930.

The picture below shows the railings to Mayfield House garden on the left, opposite the house. There was an uninterrupted view from the house across the Frome valley to Woolverton and beyond. On the skyline to the right is the first of the two tall red-brick brewery chimneys, erected in 1904.

56. Townsend looking North c1925 by Dafnis

WALK back along High Street to its junction with Lower Street.

57. The Corner House
c1900

The fronts of the buildings around the junction of Lower Street and High Street look much as they did 100 years ago, although their uses have changed with the times. On the right, in the foreground, Fussell's bakers shop is now the Cross Keys kitchen. Opposite is the former Red Lion Inn, where the inquest into the murder at Rode Hill House was opened before being transferred to the Temperance Hall.

The Corner House, built c1660, once housed the Pump Room for Rode's celebrated medicinal waters. An advertisement from a 1746 newspaper reads "Gentlemen and ladies can be supplied with Rode mineral water by sending their order to Mr Benjamin Edwards the proprietor." The single storey extension was removed when the building was restored c2000. Abutting the left wall of the Corner House is a large reddish boulder, which marked the boundary of Somerset with Wiltshire before Somerset was extended to include Rode Hill in 1937.

58. The Corner House
c1955
by Fitzwilliam

59. Topping out the New Brewhouse 1904

Henry Fussell bought the Cross Keys Inn in 1856 and began the development of a family-owned business which was to continue for a 100 years and become the major employer in the village. Adjoining the back of the Inn was the New Brewhouse (now apartments), with its two red-brick chimneys that dominate the village skyline. It was built in two stages, the first in 1904 by local builder Tom Goulter, and the second in 1935 under the direction of Henry's grandson, Percy John Fussell. Behind this was the Old Brewhouse (also converted to residential use), with its wooden-louvered upper storey where the hops were dried.

The boards on the front of the Cross Keys and the adjoining Reading Rooms listed the names of all those from the village who served in the first World War.

CONTINUE along High Street to its junction with Church Lane.

60. The Cross Keys Inn c1930

Originally called the United Counties Institute, the Reading Rooms were built by squire Batten-Pooll as a place of learning for the people of Rode and also as a celebration of Queen Victoria's Jubilee in 1887. The ground floor was divided into the main reading room, holding an extensive library, committee and games rooms. Above was a large hall for public events. To the right of the door was the caretaker's cottage.

The clock, high on the front of the building, was purchased by the villagers of Rode also to mark the Jubilee. After much debate it was decided that a large striking clock would be most fitting as it would provide a lasting visual and audible presence and be of much benefit to the village. Over £70 was collected through public subscription and £55 of this was used for its purchase.

The Reading Rooms closed in 1930 and their founder died later that year. The building was bought by Sidney Fussell & Sons Ltd, owners of the Cross Keys Inn and brewery. The ground floor became the canteen for the brewery workers but the hall above was still used for public functions.

62. The Reading Rooms c1930 by Dafnis

63. High Street
c1930
by Dafnis

The large open area, where Church Lane joins High Street, was an old market place. A market house once stood here until it was demolished in 1865. There had also been a market cross in front of it, where Wesley had preached on another of his visits to the village.

The shop on the right of the above picture belonged to Miss Toop. Some people remember her cats lying across the sweets in the window.

CONTINUE along High Street to its junction with the Big Shard, the wide path down to Lower St.

3 Hughes Court, on the corner of the Big Shard, had been a shop from at least 1843, when it was owned by Jacob Bourne. The picture below was taken when the owner was George W. Stokes. Kelly's 1898 Directory described his business as "draper, furniture dealer, grocer, provision merchant, outfitter, complete house furnisher and general factor, dressmaking, millinery and tailoring, post office".

64. G. W. Stokes'
Store
c1910

65. High Street c1925 by Wilkinson

Stokes was very active in the village - he had taken the lead in getting the Jubilee clock and was chairman of the parish council, for 30 years until he retired in 1928.

By 1927, Mrs Ethelyne Small was running the shop and from 1937 to 1945 a Mr Watt rented the business from her. After that the Central Stores as it was then called was run by the Day family; then when Lois Day married Edward Hughes in 1955, they took over.

66. E. Small's General Stores c1935

CONTINUE a little further along High Street.

*67. General Stores
Warehouse
c1935*

It was still a multipurpose store as one commentator described, "Almost any item that a household needed could be bought over the heavy mahogany counter, from a pennyworth of pear drops to a bath cap!" Hughes' Shop finally closed in 1986 and the shop and attached buildings were made into dwellings.

4 Hughes Court was used as a warehouse for the shop next door, and the ground floor of no. 5 was a garage (see above). Above them was a large L-shaped room, occasionally used for dances and other events in the days before the Memorial Hall was built.

George W. Stokes also owned these buildings and is probably where he had his furniture showroom.

*68. Stokes' Furniture
Showroom
c1910*

CONTINUE along High Street.

Opposite is the Post Office, now set back from the road, but as can be seen from the above picture, it once fronted onto the pavement.

James Goulter was a grocer/baker here as early as 1861, and it was still being used as a bakery in the 1980s. The bread ovens, embedded deep inside the building, have only recently been removed.

CONTINUE along High Street to the Village Green.

This open area was called the Pound and had a fenced area on it where stray animals were kept until claimed by their owners. Before its enclosure in 1792, Rode Common stretched right up to the pound.

70. The Pound and Christchurch c1900 by Wilkinson

71. The Pound and High Street c1900 by Wilkinson

The cottage on the left of the above picture (38 High Street), is thought to be one of the earliest remaining buildings in the village. Some of the joints of the roof timbers indicate that the oldest part is c1400.

Originally it was an open hall with an open hearth and a gallery at one end. In the 16th C. the main fireplace and chimney were put in and there are a number of other 16th and 17th C. features. In the early 18th C. it was being used as an inn, the New Inn, owned by William Stevens.

By 1777 it was called the White Hart, occupied by William George, but still owned by the Stevens family.

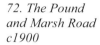

72. The Pound and Marsh Road c1900

73. Marsh Road c1935

Marsh Road is a name that dates back to the 18th C.

In the early 1800s the Poor House was there and the locals called it Poor House Lane. When the Frome Union took over responsibility for all paupers in the area, the name changed again to Union Cottage Lane until it reverted to Marsh Road at the end of the 19th C.

At the top left is Windrush, built by George W. Stokes c1926, for his retirement.

The row of 16 brick houses on the left of Marsh Road were built for the brewery workers in 1936.

74. Marsh Road c1940

*75. Box Cottage,
Pump House
and White Hart
Cottage
c1935
by Dafnis*

4 Marsh Road was built around 1650 and it is thought that no. 2, The Pump House, may have been added as a dairy. At some stage the house and dairy were divided into three dwellings, known as 1, 2 and 3 Box Cottages. By 1968 the property was almost derelict, but was saved and two cottages converted back into a single house.

The picture below, taken from the Green looking north, was incorrectly titled "Mogg Hill" on the postcard by Wilkinson. At the time, in 1900, it was called the High Street although the 1792 map of the Enclosure of Rode Common shows it as Pound Road.

76. North end of the High Street c1900 by Wilkinson

77. World War 1 War Memorial 1920

One hundred and seventy seven people from the parishes of Rode and Rode Hill served in the armed services during World War 1.

For many years after the war their names were displayed on large boards fixed to the front of the Reading Rooms and the Cross Keys Inn. 28 died in that war serving their country.

The whole community joined together to erect this memorial to them, and in 1920 it was placed on the Green, directly over the boundary line between the two parishes. It was not until 1937 that Rode and Rode Hill were officially united as one parish, within Somerset.

The picture below shows that the remains of the Pound were removed to allow the memorial to stand in serene isolation on the green.

At that time it can be seen that the Green was on the edge of the village, with nothing but Christchurch and the Vicarage between it and Rode Common.

78. The Village Green and Christchurch c1925 by Wilkinson

*79. Rode
Fair
c1905*

In the 13th C. Rode was an important settlement and Lord of the Manor, Laurence de St. Maur, obtained permission from Edward I to hold a weekly market in Rode on Thursdays and a fair on the eve, day and morrow of St. Margaret's Day. For many years, until the middle of the 19th C., a very large cheese and pleasure fair was held annually in the field called Bennersleigh, where the houses of Fairfield now stand. The field was still being used for the annual village carnival and fair as late as 1980.

The Village Green has also been the place where the community has celebrated many national events, such as coronations, jubilees and the end of major wars.

*80. Coronation
Celebrations
1953*

TO RETURN to the start of your walk, at St. Lawrence, follow Nutts Lane, next to 2 Marsh Road. At its end, turn left into Church Lane and continue to its junction with the Frome Road. Turn right past the Bell Inn and St. Lawrence is about 100 metres on the left. Take great care in crossing this busy road.

Appendix 1

Rode Time Line

1086	Domesday Survey. **Rode** is recorded as having 3 manors (parishes) and several mills
1295	**Laurence de St. Maur** obtains a grant to hold a weekly market in Rode on Thursdays and a fair on St. .Margaret's Day - 20 July
c1520	William St. Maur leaves a moiety of his remaining estates at Rode to each of his sisters – Margaret who married a **Bamwell** and Anne who married **John Stawel**
16th C.	**Benedictine Priory** (6 & 8 High Street and Habersfield House)
1559	Rode Bridge Mill built as a tucking mill
1566	**Thomas Webb** buys the Bamwell and Stawel moieties of Rode
1581	**Sir Walter Hungerford of Farleigh** acquires lands in Rode from the Zouche family
1650s	Break-up of Hungerford Estates
1705	**Henry Whitaker** builds dye factory and the **Millers House** at Rode Bridge
c1720	Old name of Rode changed to **Road** (based on wording in wills)
1730	Henry Whitaker dies and his dye factory, the Millers House and **Barrow House** pass to his son William who leases them to his brother **Thomas Whitaker**
1737	Manor of Rode bought by Mr. Andrews, Bristol merchant, and **Northfield House** (Rode Manor) built
1741	**John Batten,** clothier of **Scutt's Bridge Mill** dies
1746	John Wesley preaches under walnut tree at Townsend (south end of the High Street)
1760	**Thomas Noad,** clothier dies and his estate, including his cloth manufacturing business at **Rockabella,** passes to his protégé **Jonathan Miller** (otherwise **Noad**)
1762	Thomas Whitaker's daughters **Sally** marries Jonathan Noad; and **Rachel** marries **Samuel Ledyard**
1782	Thomas Whitaker dies and his sons-in-law; Samuel Ledyard inherits Rode Bridge estate; and Jonathan Noad inherits Shawford estate
1786	**Baptist Chapel** built
1790	**Henry Batten** dies
1790s	Cottages developed into **Southfield House** for Jonathan Noad's 1st son **Thomas Whitaker Noad**
1792	Rode Common is enclosed
1792	**Rode Hill (Langham) House** built by T. Baldwin for **Thomas Whitaker Ledyard**, son of Samuel Ledyard
1795	Jonathan Noad in residence at **Rockabella House**
1796	Manor of Rode sold to Samuel Day of Hinton
c1805	**Shawford House** developed for Jonathan Noad's 2nd son **Humphrey Minchin Noad**
1807	**John Pooll,** clothier of Scutt's Bridge Mill, and grandson of John Batten, dies
1808	Scutt's Bridge Mill occupied by brothers **Thomas** and **Henry Batten Pooll**
1808	Factory added to Rode Bridge Mill
1808	**Merfield House** built for Jonathan Noad
1809	**Methodist Chapel** built
1814	Jonathan Noad dies and leaves Merfield House to his 3rd son **Jonathan Noad**
1820	Thomas Whitaker Noad of Southfield House dies
1822	Manor of Rode and Northfield House owned by Thomas and Henry Batten Pooll
1829	Jonathan Noad dies but his wife Helen and family continue to live at Merfield

continued

Appendix 1 (continued)

Rode Time Line

1834	**National Schoolroom** opened in Langham Place
1839	**Baptist's Sunday Schoolroom** opened
1840s	Closure of Rockabella Mill
1841	**Brick Works** owned by Mrs. Emily Noad and operated by John Dunford
1851	Thomas Pooll and sister Alice are living at Merfield
1857	**Henry Fussell** acquires the Cross Keys Inn
1859	**Methodist School** built
1860	RODE HILL (Langham) HOUSE **MURDER**.
1861	Henry Batten Pooll dies at Merfield and his estate, including Northfield House, passes to his great nephew, Robert Pooll Langford, of Timsbury, on condition he changes his name to **Robert Pooll Henry Batten Pooll**
1874	Restoration of St. Lawrence, Rode
1875	Henry Fussell dies
1879	R P H Batten Pooll enlarges Northfield House and changes its name to **Rode Manor**
1886	**Sidney Fussell** acquires sole ownership of Cross Keys Inn and brewery
1887	Celebrations of Queen Victoria's golden jubilee, **United Counties Institute** founded by R. P. H. Batten Pooll and Rev. Brickmann of Christ Church opened and **Jubilee Clock** installed above window of Institute hall
1903	**S. Fussell & Sons Ltd**. builds new brew house
1904	Closure of Scutt's Bridge Mill
1913	Sidney Fussell dies and **Percy Fussell** becomes head of the brewery
1919	Order of Somerset County Council restores the spelling of **'Rode'**
1920	WW1 memorial erected on the Green
1927	Church Parishes of Rode and Rode Hill amalgamated
1928	**George W Stokes** and E Blick retire from Parish Council after 34 years service
1930	R P H Batten Pooll dies, **Walter Stewart Batten Pooll** inherits Rode Manor and lands
1930	Reading Rooms (United Counties Institute) close
1935	S. Fussell & Sons Ltd. extend 1905 brew house
1937	Civil parishes of Rode and Rode Hill amalgamated
1937	Houses for brewery employees built in Marsh Road
1953	Walter S Batten Pooll dies
1954	Rode Manor sold, much of house demolished, developed as **Tropical Bird Gardens**
1962	S. Fussell and Sons Ltd. bought out by **Bass, Mitchell and Butler**
1964	Percy Fussell dies
1966	St. Lawrence lych gate knocked down
1985	**Wesleyan Chapel** closed. Jubilee Clock restarted
1986	Central Stores closed
1991	New Scout Hut opened
1992	Brewery Distribution Depot and Cross Keys closed
1995	Christ Church closed
2000	Tropical Bird Gardens closed
2000	Village sign erected and Memorial Hall refurbished
2002	Cross Keys reopened and brewery site redeveloped
2008	Jubilee clock restored

Appendix 2

Whitaker & Noad Family Lines

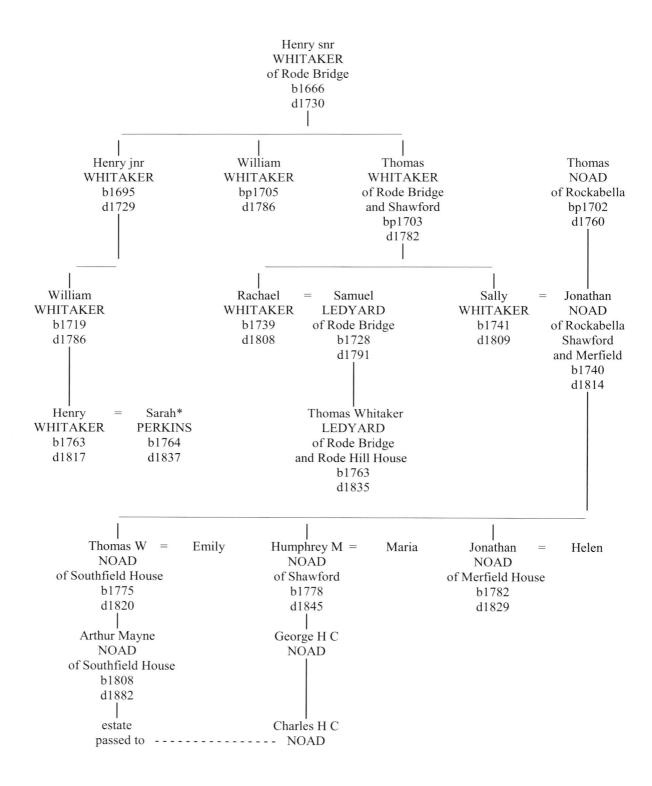

Henry snr
WHITAKER
of Rode Bridge
b1666
d1730

Henry jnr
WHITAKER
b1695
d1729

William
WHITAKER
bp1705
d1786

Thomas
WHITAKER
of Rode Bridge
and Shawford
bp1703
d1782

Thomas
NOAD
of Rockabella
bp1702
d1760

William
WHITAKER
b1719
d1786

Rachael   =   Samuel
WHITAKER   LEDYARD
b1739   of Rode Bridge
d1808   b1728
                 d1791

Sally   =   Jonathan
WHITAKER   NOAD
b1741   of Rockabella
d1809   Shawford
              and Merfield
              b1740
              d1814

Henry   =   Sarah*
WHITAKER   PERKINS
b1763   b1764
d1817   d1837

Thomas Whitaker
LEDYARD
of Rode Bridge
and Rode Hill House
b1763
d1835

Thomas W = Emily
NOAD
of Southfield House
b1775
d1820

Humphrey M = Maria
NOAD
of Shawford
b1778
d1845

Jonathan = Helen
NOAD
of Merfield House
b1782
d1829

Arthur Mayne
NOAD
of Southfield House
b1808
d1882

George H C
NOAD

estate
passed to - - - - - - - - - - - - - - -

Charles H C
NOAD

* sister of Ann, see POOLL family tree

Appendix 3

Batten & Pooll Family Lines

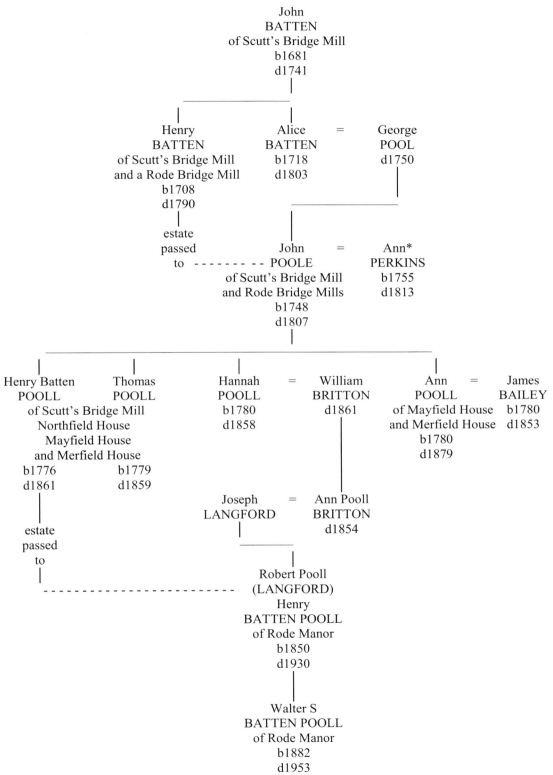

John
BATTEN
of Scutt's Bridge Mill
b1681
d1741

Henry
BATTEN
of Scutt's Bridge Mill
and a Rode Bridge Mill
b1708
d1790

estate
passed
to

Alice   =   George
BATTEN   POOL
b1718   d1750
d1803

John   =   Ann*
POOLE   PERKINS
of Scutt's Bridge Mill   b1755
and Rode Bridge Mills   d1813
b1748
d1807

Henry Batten   Thomas
POOLL   POOLL
of Scutt's Bridge Mill
Northfield House
Mayfield House
and Merfield House
b1776   b1779
d1861   d1859

estate
passed
to

Hannah   =   William
POOLL   BRITTON
b1780   d1861
d1858

Joseph   =   Ann Pooll
LANGFORD   BRITTON
               d1854

Ann   =   James
POOLL   BAILEY
of Mayfield House   b1780
and Merfield House   d1853
b1780
d1879

Robert Pooll
(LANGFORD)
Henry
BATTEN POOLL
of Rode Manor
b1850
d1930

Walter S
BATTEN POOLL
of Rode Manor
b1882
d1953

* sister of Sarah, see WHITAKER family

Appendix 4

Bibliography

General

Batten Pooll, VC., A. H., *A West Country Pot Pourri,* 1969.

Belham, P., *Villages of the Frome Area: A History,* Frome Society, 1992.

Bettey, J. H., *Rural Life in Wessex, 1500-1900,* Alan Sutton, 1977.

Bush, R., *Somerset; The Complete Guide*, 1994.

Collinson, J., *History & Antiquities of the County of Somerset,* 1791.

Farquarson, A., *History of North Bradley and Roadhill,* W. Collins, Trowbridge, 1881.

Mais, S. P. B., *Walking in Somerset,* Chambers, 1938.

Mee, A., *The Kings of England Series,* Hodder & Stoughton, 1940.

Pooley, C., *Old Stone Crosses of Somerset,* 1877.

The Victoria - History of Wiltshire volume viii - Whorwellsdown Hundred - North Bradley and Rode Hill, 1965.

Worth, R. N., *Tourist Guide to Somersetshire,* 1888

The Rode Hill House Murder

Bridges, Yseult, *Saint with Red Hands?* Jarrolds, 1954.

Chambers, P., *Murder most foul: the Road Hill House mystery of 1860,* 2009.

Kyle, N., *A greater guilt: Constance Emilie Kent and the Road Murder,* 2009

Rhode, John, *The Case of Constance Kent,* G. Bles, 1928

Somerscale, K., *The Suspicions of Mr. Whicher or The Murder at Road Hill House,* Bloomsbury, 2008.

Stapleton, J. W., *The Great Crime of 1860*, E Marlborough, 1861.

Taylor, B., *Cruelly Murdered - Constance Kent and the Killing at Road Hill House,* Grafton, 1979.